This book belongs to

_____

This book is dedicated to my children - Mikey, Kobe, and Jojo.
Try to remember to be kind to yourself, too. Self care is a priority and necessity.

Helpful Ninja

By Mary Nhin

Pictures by
Jelena Stupar

Today was the BIG day. It was Shy Ninja's season performance and she was all out of sorts.

But then, out of the corner of
her eye, she saw her friends.

It was Helpful Ninja, Inventor Ninja, and Money Ninja. They were carrying a banner that said, "You're going to do great!"

Helpful Ninja had planned it all the day before.
She had a knack for making people feel special.

She was the type of ninja that would give up her Taylor Swift concert ticket just so you could go!

Until one day, she didn't feel like helping.
Not mean. Just not as helpful and giving as
she usually was. She felt....tired.

You don't know?

Neither did her friends.

Inventor Ninja came over and concocted a special remedy.

Shy Ninja tried to help and did the
latest dance challenge for her.

But that didn't work either.

Then, Earth Ninja came over.

He brought some goodies and declared that all
Helpful Ninja needed was time for herself.

They listened to music and goofed around.

Took a nature walk and spent time outdoors.

Finally, they finished off the evening cooking Helpful Ninja's favorite pasta dish. Afterwards, she was feeling much like her old self again and thanked her friend.

Remember to guard your kind heart with plenty
of self love. You can't pour from an empty cup.

Fun, free printables at NinjaLifeHacks.tv

 @marynhin @GrowGrit
#NinjaLifeHacks

 Mary Nhin Grow Grit

 Grow Grit

CPSIA information can be obtained
at www.ICGtesting.com
Printed in the USA
LVHW072024170321
681765LV00002B/25